BOXING

BOXING

The Complete Guide to Training and Fitness

Danna Scott

A PERIGEE BOOK

A Perigee Book
Published by The Berkley Publishing Group
A division of Penguin Group (USA) Inc.
375 Hudson Street
New York, New York 10014

First edition: May 2000

Published simultaneously in Canada.

The Penguin Group (USA) Inc. World Wide Web site address is
www.penguin.com

Library of Congress Cataloging-in-Publication Data
Scott, Danna.
    Boxing : the complete guide to training and fitness / Danna Scott.—1st ed.
        p. cm.
    Includes index.
    ISBN 0-399-52601-3
    1. Boxing—Training. 2. Physical fitness. I. Title.
    GV1137.6.S36 2000

                                                                99-059079

Printed in the United States of America

18   17   16   15   14

DISCLAIMER: Every effort has been made to ensure that the information contained in this book is complete and accurate. However, neither the publisher nor the author is engaged in rendering professional advice or services to the individual reader. The ideas, procedures, and suggestions contained in this book are not intended as a substitute for consulting with your physician. All matters regarding your health require medical supervision. Neither the author nor the publisher shall be liable or responsible for any loss, injury or damage allegedly arising from any information or suggestion in this book.

Dedicated to

Julio Rivera

Special thanks to

Kay Scott, Emily Belshaw,
and Sheila M. Curry

Contents

Acknowledgments

THIS BOOK WOULD not have been possible without the help of several talented people:

Leslie Thornton, a wonderfully gifted artist and friend, did the initial photographs, including the hand-wrapping section and the author's head shot. She helped me start this remarkable project.

Robert Cardin did all the boxing and calisthenic photography. The book would not look as good as it does without his beautiful work, generosity, and expertise.

Marvin and Kay Scott were together the light at the end of the tunnel. When there was nowhere else to turn, I went to them for help, encouragement, and adverbs.

Thanks to you all!

Introduction

SEVERAL YEARS AGO I was unemployed and needed to find an inexpensive way to get in shape. A friend of mine said he was working out at Julio Rivera's Boxing Gym, so I decided to check it out. Julio had been training fighters in New York City for more than twenty-five years. His was the last boxing gym in the East Village—and also one of the cheapest.

Julio and others in the gym were friendly toward women, but to get inside you had to walk through the men's locker room, which had an open shower area and was fully visible from the ring. Big, naked, tattooed guys were a deterrent for most people, but once I passed that threshold I never stopped going back.

While pursuing an amateur boxing career, I acquired my pro cornerman's license. At the time there were only a few women cornermen in the country, but luckily that's all beginning to change, as more and more women are getting involved in the sport of boxing. As a cornerperson I worked with fighters during competitions to keep them focused and to provide strategy during the fight. First I assisted Julio, and then started cornering fights throughout New York City.

Introduction

I also began working in other clubs, training men and women in group classes as well as on a one-on-one basis. My experiences left me with extensive knowledge of the needs of both the novice and seasoned fighter. Today, my fighters range from rank beginners to Golden Glove winners and national contenders.

This book is intended for anyone who is interested in boxing at any level. Even if you never step into a ring, practicing the fundamentals of boxing can give you an excellent full-body workout that gets your legs and arms moving and your heart pumping. Boxing will also improve your stamina, help get your reflexes razor sharp, and—combined with a sensible diet—help you burn off calories. If you are looking for a great way to work out, you have come to the right place. Whether you are working out alone, with a trainer, or in a class at your local gym, this book will help you refine your skills and get the most out of your boxing workout.

For the beginner, this book offers step-by-step directions for acquiring solid boxing skills and describes training programs (see chapter 9) to get you in the best shape of your life.

If you are boxing competitively, you already know the benefits of a boxing workout. This book will give you an opportunity to perfect your skills (in both offense and defense), learn some new training routines, and improve your ring strategy.

Before you start, I suggest finding a place to work out. Look in the Yellow Pages under "Boxing Gyms." Try to talk to the owner. Tell him or her what you can afford financially and what you are looking for in a workout. He or she might give you some suggestions and even a list of trainers. Most experienced trainers, but not all, are licensed by USA Boxing (USA Boxing, United States Amateur Boxing, Inc., One Olympic Plaza, Colorado Springs, Colorado 80909, 719-578-4506, *http://www.usaboxing.org*). If you cannot find a trainer or boxing gym you like, look at local health clubs. See if there is a club that has group boxing classes. You can save money that way and also work with various trainers to see who best suits your abilities and needs.

Most gyms have gloves and hand wraps that can be borrowed, but I strongly recommend having your own basic equipment. No matter what, get your own hand wraps. They are cheap and not really something that you want to share. Also, get twelve-ounce boxing gloves for bag work; this weight of glove can also be used for initial sparring. Anything lighter might hurt your hands. You will eventually need a jump rope. I recommend plastic because it is easier to manage and cheaper than leather. You don't need boxing shoes unless you are competing; sneakers work fine. As far as clothing is concerned, T-shirts and shorts are the best choice as long as they don't restrict your movement.

Once you have your equipment and a gym, use this book to guide you through your workout. It is written in chronological order, starting with the basics of hand wrapping and going through to ring strategy and boxing styles. For the beginner, I suggest reading it in the order that it is written. For the more advanced boxer, I suggest skimming through the book, focusing on what addresses your questions as a fighter. Whatever your level, begin today to enjoy the benefits of a boxing workout!

One

BOXING EQUIPMENT

BEFORE YOU BEGIN, the following is a list of boxing equipment that you will need when you start. It starts with basic equipment for daily workouts and ends with equipment you will need for competition. If you are just beginning with boxing, start with the basics first and acquire equipment as you go along. You can ask your trainer's advice on where to get the best equipment; most gyms where boxing classes and training sessions are held also sell wraps, gloves, and so on. Check your local sporting goods store or the Internet (try searching for "boxing equipment" in any search engine), or contact manufacturers directly: Everlast, 718-993-0100 or 800-221-8777.

EQUIPMENT CHECKLIST

Equipment for daily workouts:
hand wraps
twelve-ounce leather bag gloves

Equipment for sparring:
hand wraps (same as for daily workouts)
sixteen-ounce sparring gloves
headgear
chest guard (for women)
mouthpiece
groin protector (male and female)
athletic cup (male)

Equipment for competition:
competition gauze (for hand wraps)
ten- to twelve-ounce competition gloves
mouthpiece (same as for sparring)
USA Boxing–approved headgear
chest guard (for women—same as sparring)
groin protector (same as for sparring)
athletic cup (for men—same as for sparring)
boxing trunks with opposite color waistband

Miscellaneous equipment:
jump rope
medicine ball
boxing shoes

HAND WRAPS

Hand wraps are the first thing that you need to buy, and they are also the cheapest. Wraps are usually made of cotton and range from 1 to 3 inches in width and from 120 to 170 inches long. Mexican-style wraps have elasticity in the material and give a more snug fit. If your hands are large, get the longest wrap you can find. If your hands are small, find a wrap that is not too bulky so you can make a tight fist when wrapped. Chapter 2 explains techniques for wrapping hands and how to get the best fit when you wrap.

GLOVES

Leather gloves are highly recommended. They take time to break in, but they last longer and provide better support than gloves made of synthetic materials.

Gloves come with either laces or Velcro around the wrist. Lace-up gloves fit more snugly and offer better wrist support, but they cannot be put on properly without the help of another person. Velcro gloves are best when you work alone, but they lack the support that is essential for good wrist protection.

Gloves should feel snug and be able to absorb the shock of a hard punch. Some gloves come in sizes—small, medium, and large—based on the average size of a man's hand. If you are a woman, consider the smaller sizes.

The weight of a glove varies from eight to eighteen ounces. Gloves in the twelve- to sixteen-ounce range are suggested for bag work; this way you can get a good workout without hurting your hands. If you are a heavy hitter, go for the heavier gloves. No matter what, a weekend boxer should always wear sixteen-ounce gloves.

Always spar (practice fighting with a partner) with heavy gloves, at least sixteen ounces. There is no benefit to sparring with light gloves; you can injure your hands and your sparring partner. Heavy gloves are more cumbersome and harder to hold up, but you will get a better, safer workout. All competitive fighters, whether professional or amateur, spar in sixteen-ounce gloves.

AMATEUR COMPETITION GLOVES

Depending on your weight, competition gloves range from ten to twelve ounces. The lighter the fighter, the lighter the gloves. Gloves for amateur fighters have a white knuckle area; this is the only part of the glove that can touch your opponent. At most USA Boxing–approved tournaments, gloves will be provided.

MOUTHPIECE

A mouthpiece is worn to protect a fighter's teeth, to prevent cuts to the inside of the mouth, and, most important, to protect the jaw. It gives a fighter something to clench down on to immobilize the jaw so that on impact there is less chance of injury.

It is hard to breathe with a mouthpiece in place, so give yourself time to get accustomed to it. So that it becomes a familiar piece of equipment, always work out and spar with a mouthpiece. Learn to breathe only through your nose with your mouth closed.

Each trainer has his or her own ideas about the kind of mouthpiece you should use. There are a few options. You can buy kits from which you can make your own fitted mouthpiece, or you can get a specially made mouthpiece from a dentist. Consider using a kit initially and making your own. Do not get the pre-molded plastic mouthpieces that supposedly fit all athletes. This type of mouthpiece is usually ill-fitting and extremely uncomfortable.

Make a single mouthpiece that fits only your upper teeth; that way you can clench down more easily. Breathing will be harder but a mouthpiece gives more protection for your jaw and less of a chance of being knocked out. Try different types and see which one works best for you.

HEADGEAR

A fighter should wear headgear to protect the head and ears and to lessen facial injury. Headgear is also used to protect the hands. If you are sparring with someone who is not wearing headgear, not only can you hurt your sparring partner but you can also damage your own hands, since the head is the hardest part of the body you can hit. Make sure both you and your sparring partner wear protective headgear. (Note: In many of the photos in this book the boxers are not wearing headgear for the clarity of the photos. If you spar, wear headgear!)

There are all sorts of headgear. Common sense would tell you to choose headgear that gives the most protection, but this is not always a good idea. When headgear offers too much protection, the fighter tends to stop protecting his head. The tendency is to get lazy and start dropping the hands and leading with the chin. If you are a competitive fighter, you want headgear that keeps you safe but allows you to feel the impact of a punch.

You want to get used to getting hit and learn to keep your chin down and your hands up. If you are a weekend boxer, however, use headgear that is the safest and offers the most protection.

CHEST GUARDS FOR WOMEN

Chest guards for women have become much more comfortable and efficient in recent years. Initiallty, chest guards were made of one piece of solid plastic, which was uncomfortable, hot, and cumbersome; the newer versions are lighter and have round plastic cups that fit over each breast and slide into an athletic bra. The new design is lighter and cooler, and you can breathe more easily while wearing it.

Chest guards are required for all women in competition.

GROIN PROTECTORS FOR MEN AND WOMEN

Today you can buy groin protectors for both men and women. They are designed differently for each gender. Since they protect not only the groin area but also the vital organs in the lower abdomen, it is just as important for women to wear them as it is for men. Groin protectors are heavy and hot, but they are worth the discomfort because of the protection they offer.

Men are required to wear groin protectors in all amateur and professional fights. Both men and women should always wear such protection when sparring.

JOCKSTRAPS AND FEMALE CUPS

It is a requirement that men wear a jockstrap underneath the groin protector in all competitions, and one should be worn in all sparring sessions.

Female cups are designed to provide similar protection to that of a man's cup, but they fit a woman's anatomy to add extra protection to the pubic bone. But they are not necessary for sparring or competition.

SHOES

Competition boxing shoes are designed to slide and glide across the floor while allowing for optimal movement. The high cut gives maximum support to the ankles, and the soles of the shoes are made so you can pivot easily. New styles of boxing shoes look a lot like wrestling shoes but are different in the sole. They should be used for all competition.

The downside of wearing competition shoes for workouts is that they have no arch support or cushioning for your feet. You may want to wear regular gym shoes for daily workouts, especially when jumping rope, for protection against shin splints, knee problems, and Achilles tendonitis.

BOXING TRUNKS

Boxing trunks are specifically made for boxing. The special cut of the trunks fits a man's groin protector, and the extra-wide waistband is used as a marker against low blows. You can get a less roomy version for the gym, but just any pair of old gym shorts will do for a workout.

Boxing trunks are mandatory for both men and women in competition.

CONCLUSION

If you are just starting out, the most important pieces of equipment to have are hand wraps and a good set of twelve-ounce leather bag gloves. Once you start sparring, you'll need a mouthpiece and headgear. Later, when you start heavier sparring, you'll need a groin protector and cup (if you are male). Boxing shorts and shoes aren't that important unless you are competing. Start with the basics and buy additional equipment as you need it. Some gyms sell used equipment. This is a great way to save money, but make sure used gloves aren't too worn down by checking the padding around the knuckles. If it seems too broken down, don't buy the gloves. If they are in good condition, however, buy them; used gloves in good condition are ideal because they are broken in to fit well, yet they give adequate support. Try to start small when you are buying equipment. Save your money. You don't have to spend a lot for this sport.

Two

WRAPPING YOUR HANDS

IF YOU ARE working with a trainer, the first thing he or she will do is wrap your hands. A hand wrap is a long strip of cloth that is usually made of cotton with a loop at one end and a Velcro fastener at the other. Wraps come in several different lengths to fit different-sized hands. The bigger your hand is, the longer the wrap should be.

Wrapping is technically difficult, but it is also very important, because you want to protect the delicate bones of your hands and the tendons of your wrist. Hand and wrist injuries take a long time to heal; therefore, you should take all the precautions that are available to you.

Hands should be wrapped so they feel comfortable yet supported. You should be able to make a strong, tight fist easily without cutting off circulation. Experiment with different ways to wrap your hands and then use the method that works best for you. *Always wrap your hands before a workout.*

Remember:

1. Be sure to get wraps that are a proper length, normally 120 to 170 inches long. 108-inch wraps are usually too short to provide the amount of protection a fighter needs for bag work. Wraps as long as 170 inches are sometimes too long for small hands, and the fighter is unable to make a tight fist because of too much material in the palm.

2. It is very important to spread your fingers when you are wrapping your hands, so that the wraps will be snug without cutting off your circulation. If the wraps are too tight, they will be uncomfortable and will increase your chance of injury.

3. Always start and finish wrapping at your wrist. Good wrist support is one of the most important reasons to wrap. Wrist injuries may take a long time to heal and can impair the career of a fighter.

DAILY-USE WRAPS

There are many ways to wrap hands. Here are just a few:

WRAP #1

This is one of the quickest ways to wrap your hands. It is sometimes called an amateur hand wrap. If you use short wraps, do not perform as many repetitions.

As you wrap your hands, clench and unclench your fist to check the tightness of the wrap. It should feel secure around your wrist and hand with enough give for circulation. Try to keep the wrap as smooth as possible, so it is snug but not bulky across the hand.

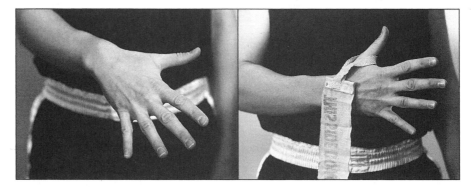

1. Spread your fingers, palm side down.
2. Put your thumb through the loop.

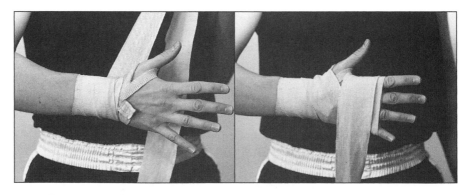

3. Wrap around your wrist three to four times.
4. Wrap across the top of your hand and wrap around your knuckles two to three times.

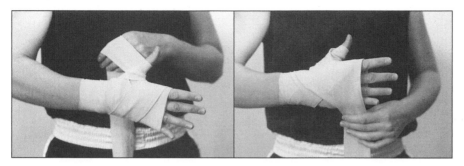

5. Wrap all the way around the base of the thumb.

6. Wrap around the knuckles once more.

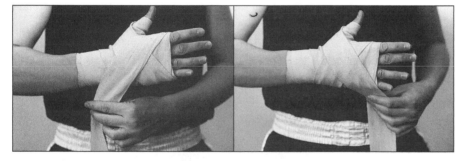

7. Do figure eights: Cross the back of the hand around the wrist, then cross around the knuckles.

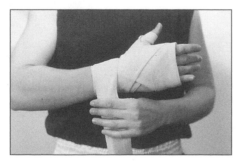

8. End at the wrist. Wrap the wrist with the remaining material and secure it with the Velcro strip.

BOXING: The Complete Guide to Training and Fitness

WRAP #2

For this technique, you will need extra-long wraps (170 to 180 inches).

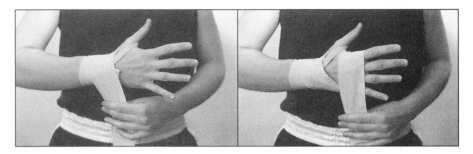

1. Spread your fingers, palm side down.
2. Put your thumb through the loop.
3. Wrap around your wrist two to three times.
4. Cross the top of your hand and wrap around your knuckles once.

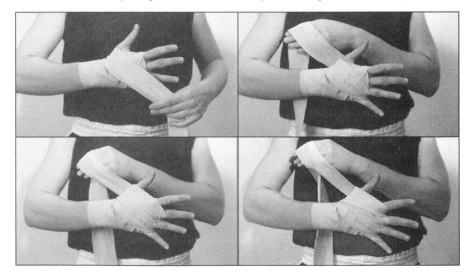

5. Wrap between your fingers using the base of the thumb as the "anchor" for the wrap: Move from the base of the thumb through the pinkie and ring finger, back around the thumb and through the ring and middle finger, then back around the thumb and through the middle and index finger.

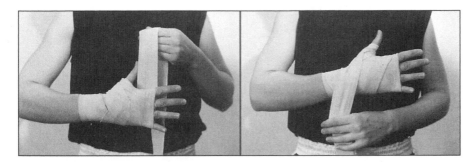

6. Wrap around the knuckles, anchoring the wrap down.
7. Wrap all the way around the base of the thumb.

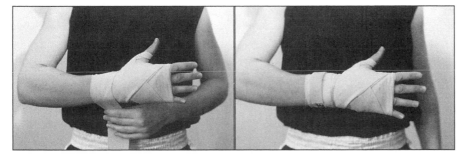

8. End at the wrist. Wrap the wrist with the remaining material and secure it with the Velcro strip.

BOXING: The Complete Guide to Training and Fitness

WRAP #3

This wrap is more easily done by a trainer, but can be carefully done by you. You'll need extra-long wraps (170 to 180 inches).

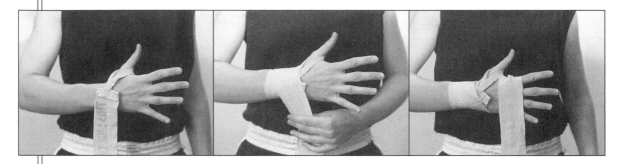

1. Spread your fingers, palm side down.
2. Put your thumb through the loop.
3. Wrap around your wrist three to four times.
4. Cross the top of your hand and wrap around your knuckles once.

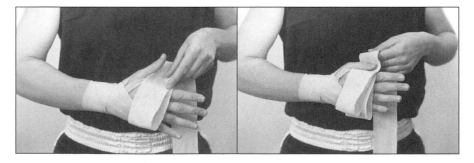

5. Make a soft, cushioned bed of cloth by laying the wrap back and forth on the knuckles, moving from pinkie to index finger several times, then stopping at the index finger.

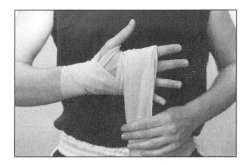

6. From the index finger, wrap all the way around your knuckles.

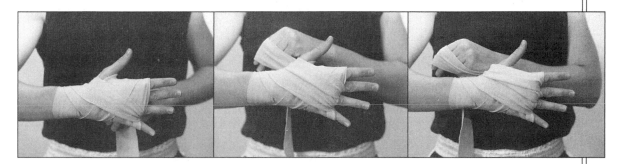

7. Go between each finger by looping around the thumb using the base of your thumb as an anchor.

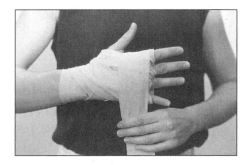

8. Wrap around your knuckles once more.

BOXING: The Complete Guide to Training and Fitness

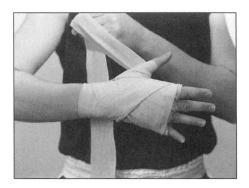

9. Wrap all the way around the base of the thumb.

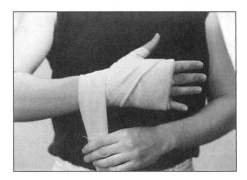

10. End at the wrist. Wrap the wrist with the remaining material and secure it with the Velcro strip.

AMATEUR COMPETITION WRAP

The difference between an amateur competition wrap and a daily-use wrap is in the materials and the amounts used. The wrap itself should be made of cotton gauze, one roll for each hand. One strip of adhesive tape measuring one by eight inches is used to secure the wrist. Two optional strips of adhesive tape criss-cross the back of the hand, securing the wrap and reaching into the palm no more than one-half inch. Tape cannot be used between the fingers, over the knuckles, across the palm, or against the skin. Wrapping may be watched over by an official and is always inspected and marked before the fight.

CONCLUSION

Wrapping is one of the first things covered in this book because it is the most important preparation you can make before a workout. When you begin to learn to box, you have the power to hit very hard, but you can get injured easily because your hands may not be strong enough to absorb the impact. Hand injuries can take an extra-long time to heal, so it's best to prevent them. Find a method of wrapping that is fast and easy for you to do. Learn to do it yourself so you can always wrap your hands whether your trainer is with you or not. Make it as natural as lacing up your shoes before a workout.

Never work out without hand wraps and always wear hand wraps and gloves whenever you spar or work the heavy bag.

Three

STANCE

BEFORE YOU THROW a punch you need to develop a good stance. A good stance allows you to put power in your punch while staying on-balance. A strong punch starts with your feet, moves up through your hips and shoulders, then releases through your fist. The more stable the stance, the more powerful the punch. A good stance will not only help you execute all your punches with optimal speed and power, but will also give you a solid base to absorb strong, hard punches from your opponent. So whether you are a power puncher throwing your punches with your feet planted or a rhythm fighter punching on the move, stance is essential.

COMMON ORTHODOX STANCE

There are many different styles of stances. Here is an example of a common orthodox style for a right-handed fighter. Left-handers do the opposite.

1. Stand with your feet hip-width apart.

2. Take a regular striding step forward with your left foot.

3. Keep your back foot at a comfortable 45-degree angle.

4. You want width and length between your feet, as if you are standing on railroad tracks.

5. Shift your weight onto the balls of your feet.

6. Distribute your weight equally between your feet.

9. Keep your knees bent.

8. Bend your elbows and tuck them into your chest.

9. Keep your fists at cheekbone level with your palms facing in. Your left hand should be slightly out in front toward your opponent, ready to throw a punch, while your right hand is tucked in at your cheekbone ready to block a punch.

10. Keep your chin down and look up.

11. Your shoulders should naturally roll forward.

12. You should be positioned partially sideways to your opponent, with your left shoulder and hand slightly closer to him or her.

13. You will use the same stance when working with punching bags.

Remember:

1. Make sure your stance is comfortable. If you feel off-balance, try again.

2. Stance is individual for each fighter. Work with your trainer to find what works for you and your body type. Don't try to copy someone else's stance. It might be wrong for you.

3. If you are right-handed, your left foot always stays forward. If you are left-handed, your right foot always stays forward. Never switch.

4. Your stance stays the same whether you are working the heavy bag, sparring, or shadow boxing.

5. Never "square off" in your stance, that is, never set your feet parallel to each other, facing your opponent with your hips and shoulders square. In this position you can be easily knocked off-balance.

6. Stance is the position from which to throw all your punches. Therefore, you want to develop a stance that is grounded yet mobile. Always keep on the balls of your feet with your knees bent and your weight distributed evenly.

BODY TYPE AND STANCE

In fighting there is a saying: "Make the taller fighter taller and the shorter fighter shorter."

If you are a taller fighter, stay more on your toes and maintain an upright stance to achieve optimal reach. This will help you stay away from your opponent's punches and capitalize on your speed. You will need to wear down your opponent before knocking him or her out. Since speed will make up for any lack of power in your punch, find a stance that allows for fast, quick movement.

If you are a shorter fighter, you should stay more in a crouch in order to be less of a target. Stay low to the ground to uproot your opponent and to get as much leverage as possible in your punches. Plant your feet solidly to maintain superior balance. Find a stance that gives you optimal power and stability in your punches.

Your stance is the source of your power and movement—so find a position that is comfortable for you.

Four

PUNCHES

IT IS VITAL to use your lower body and hips in your punch. Power generates from the balls of your feet and releases from your hips, shoulders, and finally your fist at the end of your punch. As you throw your punches think about using your whole body and not just your arms. Check out chapter 9, "Training" (page 86), to see how to practice your punches on the heavy bag.

MAKING A FIST

Making a correct fist will help you release power in your punch with the least chance of injury to your hands.

1. Start with your fingers outstretched.

2. Roll your four fingers into the palm of your hand, making a tight ball.

3. Tuck your thumb along the outside of your index finger. *Never tuck your thumb inside your fist or you could break it during a punch.*

4. Your fist should form a solid flat surface to hit with, lining up the major knuckles of your hand at the point of impact. Make sure your fist is tight, with your fingers rolled into your palm as snug as possible. You want the hard knuckles of your hand to feel the impact of your punch, not your fingers.

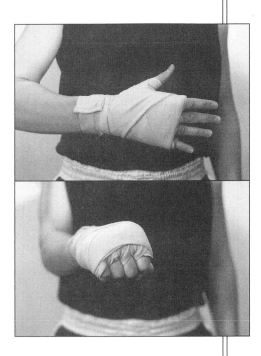

Remember:

1. You can test the fist of one hand by hitting the palm of your other hand. It should make a resounding smack.

2. Your fist and wrist should be as strong as possible when you punch. You can develop these areas by squeezing a small ball and by doing wrist curls with three- to five-pound weights. (Hold the weight in your hand with your forearm outstretched, palm down. Using your wrist lift the weight twenty times with each hand.)

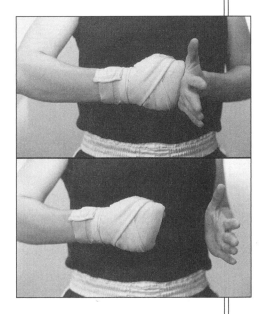

BASIC PUNCHES

The instructions for punches in this chapter are written for right-handed fighters. If you are left-handed substitute left for right in all instructions.

Remember:

1. Make sure you have a straight wrist and a tight fist in your glove.

2. Keep your upper body loose with your hands up and chin down.

3. Stay relaxed in your head, neck, and shoulders.

READY POSITION

Before you throw a punch, make sure you are in ready position. It is the starting point for all your punches.

1. Get into your correct stance, with your right foot forward and your left foot back.

2. Make a proper fist and bring your hands up to cheekbone level.

3. Keep your elbows tucked and your chin down.

4. Shift your weight to the balls of your feet and keep your knees bent.

JAB

The jab is thrown with the lead hand. Right-handed fighters throw their jab with their left hand and left-handed fighters jab with their right hand. The jab is used to find your reach and to force your opponent off-balance. The jab is rarely a knockout punch, but it can help you set up power punches, such as the straight right or left hook.

Jabbing in a Planted Position

1. From your basic stance, snap your left arm out with a slight pivot of your hip and shoulder.

2. Rotate your left shoulder so that your punch lands with your palm facing downward.

3. Snap your jab back into the ready position.

Stepping into Your Jab:

1. From your basic stance, drive off the ball of your right foot.

2. Step forward with your left foot.

3. Snap your left hand outward, rolling your shoulder over so your punch lands with your palm facing down.

4. Your right foot glides across the floor into position as your punch makes contact.

6. Snap the jab back to the ready position.

Remember:

1. Don't lead with your elbow. It should never stick out away from your body during any part of the punch.

2. Punch in a straight line. Don't drop your left during execution or on the way back to the ready position.

3. Keep your right hand up. The right stays at cheekbone level throughout your jab to protect your chin.

STRAIGHT RIGHT

For right-handers, the straight right is your power punch (for left-handers, your power punch is the straight left). This punch has power because of the extra torque from your hips and shoulders.

1. From your basic stance, screw the ball of your back foot into the ground as if you're putting out a cigarette.

2. Turn your right hip and shoulder toward your opponent.

3. As you extend your punch, rotate your shoulder and forearm counterclockwise so that your punch lands knuckles up, palm down.

4. Keep extending your punch as if you are punching *through* your opponent, not *at* him.

5. When your punch is fully extended, release completely through your shoulder, but don't lock your elbow.

6. Using the momentum of your punch, snap your right hand back into the ready position.

Remember:

1. Always keep your chin down.

2. Don't drop your left while you're throwing your right.

3. Don't pull your right hand back (or cock it) before you execute your punch or you will telegraph your intent to your opponent.

LEFT HOOK

The left hook is generally a hard punch to learn for right-handers because you are usually less coordinated using your left hand. In addition, coming from your customary stance, you may find it harder to generate power from your hips. If done right, however, the left hook is a strong and effective punch that can be used to hit the side of your opponent's head or her body and can be fully executed outside her field of vision. If your opponent has her hands up, her right hand will obscure her peripheral vision and she won't see the left hook coming.

1. From your basic stance turn your hips and shoulders to your left.

2. Screw your front foot into the ground, as if you're putting out a cigarette.

3. Roll your shoulder so that your punch lands parallel to the floor

with your arm at a 90-degree angle. Your punch should land with your palm facing in and your knuckles out or with your palm facing down and your knuckles up.

4. Your back foot should remain planted, working as an anchor.

5. Using the momentum from your punch, bring your left hand back to the ready position.

Remember:

1. Don't throw wild (roundhouse) blows or you will drop your defense and leave yourself wide open to your opponent's counterpunches.

2. Don't overextend your punch. You do not want your punch to go beyond a 90-degree angle.

3. Don't drop your right hand when you throw your left hook.

RIGHT HOOK

The right hook is thrown exactly like the left hook but with the right hand. Stay in the same boxing stance with your left foot forward. Power comes off your right foot, with your left foot used for stability.

The right hook is not as essential as the left hook. The straight right can take care of anything that you would need the right hook for, and you are less vulnerable to being hit.

UPPERCUTS

The uppercut can be thrown with either hand at medium to short range and is particularly effective when thrown in close quarters. Uppercuts can be thrown to the body or to the head. They work well against short crouching opponents to upright them and against tall opponents to get under their reach.

Left Uppercut

1. From your basic stance, turn your hips and upper torso to your left.

2. Bend your knees and shift your weight to your front (left) foot.

3. Angle your left shoulder downward.

4. Drive off the ball of your front foot through your left hip and release through your punch.

5. Land your punch with an upward motion, a short arc, palm facing up, with your wrist firm and straight.

6. Use the momentum of your punch to bring your hand back and into position.

Right Uppercut

1. From your basic stance, turn your hips and torso to your right.

2. Dip your right shoulder down to your right.

3. Drive off your back foot through your right hip and release through your punch.

4. Land your punch with an upward motion, palm facing up with your wrist firm and straight.

5. Using the momentum of your punch, bring your hand back into the ready position.

Remember:

1. Don't bend at the elbow before executing your uppercut or you will telegraph your intent to your opponent.

2. Don't lead with your chin. Keep your chin down so you don't open up on your punch.

3. Keep your wrist straight. If you bend your wrist on impact you could damage the tendons in that area.

PRACTICING YOUR FORM

During your first six months of training, work on form. Practice in front of a mirror so you can see if your punches are technically correct. Then, work on the heavy bag, practicing one punch at a time. Find ways to generate power, but remain on balance. Check chapter 9, "Training" (page 86), for further suggestions on your workout.

Five

MOVEMENT (Footwork)

MOVEMENT IS BOTH offensive and defensive. You need to be able to move easily in all directions to be able to keep out of your opponent's reach as well as to get close enough to land punches. The most important thing to remember about footwork is that when you move in any direction, your body weight should remain centered and balanced. Stay on the balls of your feet, but not too high on your toes, so you can move easily but maintain your stability. The foot that is closest to the direction you are going moves first. For example, when you move forward, your front foot moves first and your back foot follows. This way, your feet never get any closer to each other than in your basic stance and they never cross over each other.

VERTICAL MOVEMENT

MOVING FORWARD

Forward movement indicates an offensive maneuver. As you are stepping forward, keep jabbing and setting up for a power punch, such as a straight right. Keep your chin down and stay low.

1. From your basic stance, push off the ball of your back foot.

2. Step forward with your front foot one half step.

3. Follow with your right foot, moving forward one half step; this brings you back to your basic stance.

MOVING BACKWARD

When moving backward, you are in a defensive posture. Look for an opening and throw power punches to the body to slow your opponent down. It is good to be able to move backward, but don't depend on such movement, especially against a stronger fighter. If you do, you may end up being pushed back against the ropes, where you can be overwhelmed by your opponent.

1. From your basic stance, push off the ball of your front foot.

2. Step backward with your back foot one half step.

3. Follow with your left foot, moving backward one half step. You are now back to your basic stance.

LATERAL MOVEMENT

MOVING LEFT

Most right-handed boxers find it easier to move to their left, since they will be stepping into their jab. Moving to the left is also a good direction to take when you are fighting a left-handed boxer because you will be moving away from his power.

1. From your basic stance, push off the ball of your right foot.

2. With your left foot, move one half step to the left.

3. Follow with your right foot, moving to the left one half step.

BOXING: **The Complete Guide to Training and Fitness**

MOVING RIGHT

Moving to your right is just like moving left, but more awkward because you won't be able to step as easily into your jab. Moving to the right will help you avoid your opponent's right hand, but you can be readily hit with her left hook. Obviously, you want to learn to move in either direction with ease.

1. From your basic stance, push off the ball of your left foot.

2. Move with your right foot one half step to the right.

3. Follow with your left foot, one half step to the right.

SHUFFLING

TO THE RIGHT AND TO THE LEFT

Shuffling right and left is a good way to get away from your opponent instead of backing up. When you shuffle right, you avoid your opponent's left hook. When you shuffle to the left, you avoid his straight right. Learn to go in either direction and practice switching directions quickly. As your opponent moves toward you in a straight line, shuffle in a circular motion around him. Mix up directions so your opponent won't have time to set up for his punches.

1. Bring your feet hip-width apart and parallel and your hips and shoulders square to your opponent. (This is the only time you ever want to be square to your opponent: when you are moving away from your opponent—and away from danger. Never stop moving—but if you do stop, step into your stance to throw a strong, hard punch.)

2. Shuffle to the left by pushing off your right foot and stepping with your left, never letting your feet come closer than hip-width apart.

3. Shuffle to the right by pushing off your left foot and stepping with your right.

4. Change directions quickly and often so you can stay away from your opponent's power.

PIVOTING

Pivoting is used when you want to change the angle of approach to your opponent so you can set up better for counterpunching (counterpunching is simply defensive punching). It works well with other defensive moves, such as bobbing and weaving and slipping (see chapter 7, "Defense," page 64).

1. Get into your boxing stance.

2. Shift your weight to the ball of your front foot.

3. Push off your back foot and pivot on your front foot a quarter turn to the right or left.

4. You should be back in your boxing stance, but at a 90-degree angle to your opponent.

Remember:

1. Always try to counterpunch after pivoting. You are in an excellent position to do so; don't pass up a great opportunity.

2. Practice all your footwork in front of a mirror and in the ring.

Six

COMBINATIONS

AFTER LEARNING TO throw strong, hard, single punches, you must next learn to throw combinations. A combination is a series of punches thrown in rhythm without hesitation. Each punch should flow naturally into the next to maintain speed, balance, and power. Even in a good fight, only about a third of the punches you throw will actually hit your opponent; therefore, by throwing combinations you have more of a chance of making contact. Remember, your opponent is trying to avoid being hit by blocking and slipping your punches (chapter 7, "Defense," page 64). The more punches you throw, therefore, the more likely you are to hit your target.

COMMON COMBINATIONS

In combinations, certain punches are commonly represented by certain numbers: a left jab is represented by the number one; a straight right is two; a left hook is three; a right uppercut is four; and a left uppercut is five. Different trainers may use different combinations of numbers to describe basic punches.

LEFT JAB–STRAIGHT RIGHT
(One-Two) Combination

Commonly known as "the ol' one-two," this is a simple combination that leads, or starts, with the left jab and ends with a straight right. This is the first combination you should learn. Like most combinations, the left jab sets you up to throw a power punch, in this case your straight right.

1. Set up your combination with your left jab.

2. As your jab snaps back to the ready position, throw a strong right hand.

3. After making contact, bring your right back, with both hands at cheekbone level.

Remember:

Don't underestimate the importance of this elementary combination. Many fighters have built careers on its perfect execution. Muhammad Ali is a prime example of a fighter who relied heavily on coordinating these two simple punches.

LEFT JAB-STRAIGHT RIGHT-LEFT HOOK
(One-Two-Three Combination)

This is a classic combination and a more difficult one. It requires solid coordination because you begin and end the combination with your left hand. The beauty of this combination, however, is that by throwing a left hook after a strong right, you should have good balance. When you end with a left hook, you are less vulnerable to counterpunches. In fact, you should consider ending all of your combinations with your left hand since that will put you in a better position to throw other combinations with less chance of getting hit. This one-two-three combination is bread and butter to a successful fighter. Once the balance and coordination are worked out, you can build up to more difficult combinations.

1. Step into your left jab, snapping it out and back.

2. Throw your straight right.

3. Screw the ball of your front foot into the ground, as if you're putting out a cigarette, and throw a left hook to the head.

Your straight right will put your hips in perfect position to throw a left hook. Make sure your weight stays centered and shifts forward for your hook. Both the straight right and the left hook should be used as power punches. What the straight right doesn't take care of, the left hook will.

LEFT JAB–LEFT HOOK
(One-Three Combination, or "Hooking Off Your Jab")

This combination is called "hooking off your jab." It is important to learn to throw several punches with the same hand; this way you can mix up the angles and rhythms of your punches to confuse your opponent.

Hooking off your jab can be followed by more complicated combinations by adding your straight right.

1. Execute a left jab first; then bring your left arm halfway back.

2. Screw the ball of your front foot into the ground as if you're putting out a cigarette, and roll your left shoulder to throw a left hook immediately to your opponent's head.

3. End with hands at cheekbone level.

LEFT JAB-LEFT HOOK TO THE HEAD-STRAIGHT RIGHT

This combination is a variation of the one-two-three combination, but here you are hooking off your jab and then ending with a strong knockout punch to the head.

1. Throw your left jab.

2. Bring your jab halfway back and throw a left hook to the head.

3. Immediately throw a strong straight right to the head.

4. End with both hands at cheekbone level.

BODY PUNCHES IN COMBINATIONS

It is important after throwing a body shot to end with a head shot. It is human nature for your opponent to drop her hands slightly after being hit in the body. Real pain can be inflicted by throwing strong hard punches to the vital organs of the lower body. Such punches will force your opponent into an upright stance and will open her up for a shot to the head.

All the body shots in the following combinations are either thrown up the middle of your opponent's body (at the sternum) or hooked to the body (at the kidneys). In either case these are excellent combinations to use when your opponent is up against the ropes.

RIGHT UPPERCUT TO THE BODY-LEFT UPPERCUT TO THE BODY-DOUBLE LEFT HOOK TO THE CHIN

This is a great combination to confuse your opponent, since tripling up with your left hand will be an unexpected maneuver.

1. Step in and throw your right and left uppercuts to the body.

2. Immediately turn your hips slightly to the left and throw a double left hook to the head.

Remember:

For your body shots keep your chin down. Get leverage from bending your knees, staying low, and thrusting from your hips.

LEFT UPPERCUT TO THE BODY-RIGHT UPPERCUT TO THE BODY-LEFT HOOK TO THE HEAD-STRAIGHT RIGHT TO THE HEAD

This is great to throw when your opponent is cornered against the ropes.

1. Step in and throw right and left uppercuts to the body.

2. Throw a strong left hook to the head.

3. Bring home your right hand with all its power to your opponent's chin.

LEFT HOOK TO THE BODY-LEFT HOOK TO THE CHIN-STRAIGHT RIGHT

This three-punch combination is quick and easy, and it works.

1. Step in and to the side and throw a left hook to the body.

2. Bring your left hand back, screw the ball of your front foot into the ground, roll your shoulder over, and throw a left hook to the chin.

3. Step back and throw a straight right.

Remember:

1. Always throw something to the head after throwing body shots before moving away from your opponent. This keeps him busy and off balance.

2. When throwing your punches, aim at specific areas of the body. When throwing a body shot, either go up the middle (to the sternum) or hook to the side (to the kidneys). When throwing a left jab or straight right, aim for the nose. A left or right hook to the head should aim for the temple or side of the jaw. When throwing uppercuts to the head, throw up the middle of the body to the jaw. If you are specific about the placement of your punches, they will have more effect.

CONCLUSION

When you practice your combinations, start slowly. Get into a rhythm for each combination so the punches flow smoothly. Do not pause in between each punch, but move from one punch to the next. Start with simple combinations and build up to three- and four-punch combinations. Remember to move after each combination so you won't get hit when your opponent tries to retaliate. When boxing for fitness, throwing combinations at a bag or shadowboxing in front of a mirror will give you a great workout.

Seven

DEFENSE

BEING A COMPLETE boxer is not just about hitting but also about *not* getting hit. In his early pro career, Mike Tyson, who was feared for his pure aggression, was also an extremely effective defensive boxer. Not only could he hit his opponent with the strongest punches in the business, but rarely could anyone hit him back. His style has changed in recent years, and he is no longer the defensive fighter he used to be. He is now much more vulnerable in the ring. Don't allow yourself to be vulnerable to your opponent's punches. If you want to be a successful fighter, you must be smart; be as conscientious in learning defense as you are in learning offense.

BASIC DEFENSE

BLOCKING

Blocking is the simplest of all the defensive moves and the most natural. While it doesn't allow your hands to remain free to counterpunch, it is a move that can be used against all the basic punches. Learn it first as you begin building your defensive repertoire.

1. Block left hooks by using the outside of your glove and forearm, with your hand raised above your temple. *Don't stick your arm or elbow out to meet the punch.*

2. Block hooks to the body by tucking your arm in and down to block with your elbow or forearm.

3. Defend against body shots up the middle by dropping your arm parallel to the floor at a 90-degree angle, blocking the punch with the inside (palm side) of your glove.

Remember:

1. When blocking a head shot, don't reach for the punch or you will open yourself up as a target for your opponent. Keep your elbows down and your arms tucked in.

2. Keep your fists at least four inches away from your face, so if you do block a punch you won't get jolted by your own glove.

DUCKING

Ducking is used most effectively against a straight right or a left hook. It tends to be too slow against a jab. With both hands free you are capable of counterpunching (defensive punching) to the body. Ducking gives you the opportunity to throw a strong left to the stomach because you can use the downward momentum from your legs for power.

1. Duck head shots by bending deep in your knees and keeping your chin down.

2. Don't look at the floor; keep your eyes on your opponent.

3. Duck low enough to go directly underneath your opponent's punch while maintaining your balance sufficiently to counterpunch.

PARRYING

Parrying is used against straight head shots; it is a defensive move that is done with the open palm of your glove. You catch the punch and swipe it down or to the side. The movement of your hand is very small, just enough to change the direction of the punch. Your hand should stay as close to cheekbone level as possible.

1. Parry a left jab using the open glove of your right hand to swipe it down or to the right side, away from your face.

2. Parry a straight right with your left hand to swipe it down and to the side away from your face.

Remember:

You can parry and counterpunch off the same hand—for example, parrying with your left hand, then throwing a left jab.

ROLLING

The psychology of this movement is different from any other defensive maneuver. When rolling with a punch, you are actually getting hit but minimizing its power by "yielding" with the shot. You do not want to meet power with power; you want to roll with it. In other words, you are allowing your opponent to punch you, but you are taking the sting out of the punch by yielding with the momentum of the punch. Rolling can look a lot like blocking, but you are actually turning your body more in the direction that the punch is going, to absorb its power.

1. Roll with a right head shot by turning your body to the right, bending your knees slightly, and taking the punch with your left upper arm and shoulder.

2. Roll with a left hook to the head by turning your body to the left, bending your knees slightly and taking the punch with your right upper arm and shoulder.

3. Roll with a right body shot by tucking your left elbow in, bending your waist down on the right side, and turning in the direction that the punch is going.

Remember:

1. Always roll in the direction that the punch is going.

2. If you have to take a shot, try to take it on your shoulder and upper arm.

BOXING: **The Complete Guide to Training and Fitness**

BOBBING AND WEAVING

By bobbing and weaving, you are making a U shape with the movement of your upper body. As your opponent throws her punch, bend at the knees and slip underneath the punch, coming up on the other side. You can bob and weave either from the inside to the outside or from the outside to the inside of the punch. Always keep your eyes on your opponent. Never look down, even if you are getting hit. Bobbing and weaving is a very slow method of defense, and therefore doesn't always work. Make sure to keep your hands up and bend your knees so you can take some of the power off a punch if you get hit.

1. Bob and weave from the inside of a left hook by bending your knees and slipping under the punch.

2. Come up on the outside of your opponent's reach.

Remember:

Bobbing and weaving comes from bending your legs with only a slight bend at the waist. If you bend too much at the waist, you will be penalized in an amateur fight.

SLIPPING

Slipping is one of the most difficult and dangerous defensive moves in boxing. It is best used when your opponent is throwing his jab or straight right. The advantage to slipping a punch is that you have two hands free to counterpunch. To slip, you must be extremely quick and agile. If you are a slow fighter, slipping may not be appropriate for your style. However, you should learn slipping so that you have it in your arsenal of defenses.

1. To slip a jab, bend at the waist and knees.

2. Lean slightly forward to the inside or outside of the punch, keeping your chin down and hands up.

3. Your body should shift so that your opponent's punch lands past your head and over your shoulder.

Remember:

1. Slipping is subtle, and you want to slip only enough to avoid getting punched. This ensures better balance for counterpunching.

2. You can slip either to the outside or to the inside of a punch. If you slip to the inside, you have a bigger target to hit, but you must counter immediately. Slipping outside is safer, but your opponent is then more difficult to hit.

3. Sometimes an opponent will feint (fake a punch) with one hand and hit you with the other, and you will end up slipping the wrong way and into your opponent's punch. Always keep your hands up so if you make a mistake, you can block part of her punch with your glove.

ALI LEAN (SNAP BACK OR SWAY BACK)

This defensive move is used against straight head shots. The Ali lean is a dangerous maneuver that can be used only if your feet provide a wide enough base, with a strong back leg for balance.

1. Drop your weight back onto the ball of your back foot.

2. Tuck your chin down and keep your eyes on your opponent as you make a slight curve in your back.

3. After your opponent misses, use the momentum of your movement to spring forward and counterpunch. *When you are first trying this maneuver, counter with a jab and later find your range with a straight right.*

Remember:

The Ali lean is not suited to every fighter. Agility and quickness are essential. This move works best for tall, lean, fast fighters with superb coordination and conditioning.

CLINCHING

Clinching is done when you are tired or hurt and need time to collect yourself. It is used mostly as a defensive move, but often an inside fighter will use a clinch offensively to tie up his opponent and get in a couple of shots. Well-timed clinches can wear down your opponent to your advantage.

1. To clinch, reach around your opponent's shoulders, then slide down her arms until you reach her elbows.

2. Wrap your elbows around your opponent's arms.

3. Lay your head on the left shoulder of your opponent to rest and to avoid illegal head butts.

4. Lean all your weight on your opponent so she is essentially holding you up with her legs.

Remember:

Clinching is not well liked in amateur fights. You can get warned for clinching or even penalized if you do it too much. So use clinching sparingly and only when necessary.

GETTING OUT OF A CLINCH

1. Before your opponent ties you up, throw body punches up the middle to back him up. This will move his head off your shoulder so you can throw shots to the head. If you do get completely tied up, as the photo shows, then lay your head on your opponent's shoulder and lean all your body weight on him. Try to rest until the referee breaks you up.

2. Move away from him at an angle, *never straight back*. Keep your hands up because your opponent might try to punch once you've broken contact.

To avoid getting into a clinch, step back and throw a right to the head.

Remember:

Do not bear-hug. It is the least effective way to clinch and it works only when you are bigger and stronger than your opponent. If you are bigger and stronger, you shouldn't need to be doing this type of clinching in the first place.

COVERING UP

Covering up is done when you are so overwhelmed that you are unable to counterpunch or even clinch. Often at this point you are backed up against the ropes and have no other options but to protect yourself from being hit.

Double Arm Cover

When you use the double arm cover you are no longer able to actively defend yourself. You are just taking the punches and riding out the storm. It is usually done when you are hurt and are just saving yourself from further punishment. This maneuver can sometimes work in pro fights to wear down your opponent. But there is no time to wear down your opponent in an amateur fight. There are only three rounds and the refereeing is much more conservative. If a ref sees that you are not answering your opponent's punches he will stop the fight.

1. To use the double arm cover, tuck your chin down and roll your shoulders forward.

2. Keep your hands up with your elbows tucked into your body as much as possible.

3. Create a space between your gloves to see your opponent and to look for an opportunity to counterpunch.

4. Keep your knees bent, sit back on the ropes, and try to rest while absorbing your opponent's punches.

Half Cover

This is a modified cover.

1. Keep your left arm high—at temple level—to protect your face.

2. Keep your right arm low—at waist height, parallel to the floor—to protect your body.

3. Roll your right shoulder forward and tuck your chin in.

Cross-Arm Guard, or Armadillo Defense

This particular blocking technique looks primitive, but it will get the job done against a taller opponent. If you are a short fighter with a good left hook, this is a good defensive posture. With this guard, you can press forward by bobbing and weaving and get under your opponent's defenses to counter to the body.

Archie Moore perfected the armadillo defense, which became popular with other boxers in the 1950s.

1. Get into a low crouch.

2. Cross your arms over, with your left on top and parallel to your right.

3. Keep your left arm up, protecting your chin (at about a 45-degree angle to the floor).

4. Keep your right arm underneath your left arm parallel to the floor. When you use this guard correctly, your forearms and the top of your head should be the only targets left for your opponent.

Remember:

The left arm protects your chin while the right arm protects the body.

CONCLUSION

The best way to learn defense is to spar. You can hone your skills by shadowboxing and working with your trainer, but nothing beats sparring for giving one a true understanding of defensive moves. Find a sparring partner that you can trust, who won't hit you too hard but but will hit you hard enough to keep you alert. Don't go too soft or you'll never really learn how to defend against a strong punch.

As a beginner, just try to keep your head moving and use basic blocking techniques. If you do these two things, and do them well, you should be able to get out of most difficult situations. When you feel ready, start parrying and bobbing and weaving; you can learn the more difficult moves later. Take your time. It's better to do a few things well than a lot of things halfway—a sure way to lose a fight. Make certain your sparring partner doesn't punch too fast or too hard, you want to build your confidence, not lose it.

Eight

RING STRATEGY and BOXING STYLES

WHEN YOU FIGHT, you put together your movement and punches as well as use the movements of your opponent and the actual ring itself to gain an advantage in a fight.

BASIC RING STRATEGY

CUTTING OFF THE RING

Cutting off the ring is a way of making the ring smaller. The goal is to get your opponent against the ropes, within range of your punches, by keeping him from circling left or right.

1. When your opponent circles to his left, step in a straight line to your right.

2. When your opponent circles to his right, step in a straight line to your left.

3. Keep moving forward, driving him back.

4. When your opponent starts moving backward and ends up against the ropes, move to the inside throwing strong body shots; then go to the head.

Remember:

When your opponent tries to circle, move in a straight line to cut him off.

FIGHTING ON THE ROPES

1. If you are forced up against the ropes, it is important to stay low.

2. Keep your back leg bent.

3. When your back leg hits the lower rope, lean forward on your front foot to get leverage.

4. Throw hard body shots up the middle and try to press forward off the ropes, or pivot.

Remember:

Don't end up flat-footed and upright against the ropes, or you will be unable to move. If this does happen, sit back on the ropes and use the give of the ropes to absorb punches. This is not an optimal position to be in, and you could get penalized for it in an amateur fight. Try to ride out the storm. Wear your opponent down and get a few punches in at the end of the round.

PIVOTING OFF THE ROPES

When you are forced back against the ropes, it is sometimes possible to pivot around your opponent and get off the ropes.

1. When your opponent has you up against the ropes, cup his right elbow in your left glove.

2. Lean forward to your left and shove his elbow out while you pivot at a 90-degree angle.

3. Once you have pivoted off the ropes, throw a strong right hand to the head.

Remember:

1. When pivoting off the ropes, you can control your opponent by shoving his elbow forward or by placing your hand on the small of his back and pushing him forward.

2. You can pivot in both directions. Using this technique, you can pivot off the ropes cupping his left elbow in your right glove and pivoting to your right.

BOXING STYLES

THE LONG-RANGE BOXER

The term *boxer* is used for a fast-moving fighter who works outside her opponent's reach but stays just close enough to make contact with her own punches. She uses the ring to circle in both directions around her opponent, and the bigger the ring the better. A long-range boxer is usually a tall, lanky fighter with a long, lean build. She does not necessarily have a knockout punch, but relies on her hand speed and superior reach to frustrate her opponent. Her jab is her most effective weapon. She uses it offensively as well as defensively, scoring points for every punch she lands. (Remember, amateur fights are won mostly on points. Each time you hit your opponent, you score the same number of points whether you hit her soft or hard. A jab, therefore, scores as much as a knockdown.)

A long-range fighter generally moves left, stepping into her jab to maintain good footwork. Staying on the balls of her feet in an upright stance enhances her long reach and fast footwork. She also aims to keep her body at a slight angle, with her left foot stepping between her opponent's feet to prevent the opponent from boring in. When the long-range boxer's reach is penetrated, she uses a clinch to avoid getting hit in the body.

This type of fighter usually scores well in amateur bouts, fighting at a very fast pace. The very nature of this fighting style, however, leads to a shorter pro career, since the first thing to go with age is speed, and speed is what a boxer needs to survive.

Fighting a Long-Range Boxer

Keep the pressure on and, above all, don't get frustrated. Let her wear herself out. Slow down the pace, cut off the ring, but don't chase her. Stay in a low crouch so the taller fighter must punch down. Move from side to side in both directions. Slip under her jab and work the body. Once you have gotten in some good body shots, go for the head. Keep your head down and stay low. Try to force the boxer into standing and exchanging punches.

THE INFIGHTER

An inside fighter is usually a forward-moving stalker who knows how to cut off the ring. He may not be fast or have fancy footwork, but he fights from a low, hard-to-penetrate stance. This type of fighter is usually short with a square build; thick, strong muscles; and a low center of gravity. The inside fighter can slip under his opponent's reach and throw hard body and head shots. He is usually a heavy puncher. He should be in extremely good shape and have a natural killer instinct plus a strong chin. His natural ability to take a punch serves him well, since he may have to take a few to get inside his opponent's reach. This type of fighter usually has a long professional career, but not necessarily an outstanding amateur one, because amateur scoring tends to favor long-range boxers.

Fighting an Infighter

Don't be intimidated. Move from side to side. Keep him away with your jab. Being a moving target will keep him off balance and unable to set up for his punches. Do not try to exchange punches with him. When he tries to attack, pivot and counterpunch. Think of him as the bull and yourself as the matador.

THE COUNTERPUNCHER

A counterpuncher lets her opponent throw the first punch and then goes on the attack after her opponent has committed himself. This is a very difficult style to master. It requires excellent defense, footwork, reaction time, and conditioning. A counterpuncher is usually of medium build and works within the medium range of her opponent. She knows all the tricks to drawing out her opponent (making her opponent throw the first punch). She knows how to feint (bluff) her punches and purposely lower her guard so her opponent will attack. Yet, she has enough hand speed to be able to block and then counterattack.

Fighting a Counterpuncher

Beat her at her own game. Draw her into leading an attack by feinting with your punches; then outpunch her. Counter her counterattacks and keep her under pressure so that she is unable to set up. Constant sparring and working on the double-end bag will help develop the reflexes needed to counter the counterpuncher.

THE SOUTHPAW (Left-Hander)

A southpaw has a distinct advantage over his opponent because everything he does is the opposite of what is expected. Fighting a left-handed fighter is difficult even for another left-hander. Southpaws tend to be natural counterpunchers, waiting for their opponent to make a mistake and then going in for the kill. Often an opponent will simply walk right into a strong left hand. Left-handers usually do well in amateur fights because by the time their opponent figures out their style, the fight is over.

Fighting a Left-Hander

When fighting a lefty, remember to move constantly to *your* left and away from his power. Throw left hooks, hook off your jab, and lead more with your right. Practice sparring with left-handers. Get used to them. Nothing beats experience.

CONCLUSION

The best way to develop good ring strategy is to start competing in the ring. Nothing beats fighting under pressure. A lot of your strategy will come from your trainer before the fight and between rounds.

Be aware that this information on boxing styles is broad and general. Try not to make assumptions about your opponent. A tall, lean fighter might be a brawler. A short, squat fighter might try to jab and move. Sometimes fighters mix up styles to confuse their opponent. You should learn to mix up styles as well. If you are tall, practice planting your feet and throwing knockout punches. If you are short, jab and move. You will then be able to successfully use these unexpected moves against your opponent.

Nine

TRAINING

BOXING TRAINING IS a great cardiovascular workout. It also develops strong, long, lean muscles and fast reflexes. Because it is such a good all-around workout that emphasizes hand-eye coordination and conditioning, it works well in cross-training for other sports, such as tennis and basketball.

Boxing can get you in the best shape of your life, but you must be disciplined. The better shape you are in, the less likely you are to get hurt. Exhaustion can lead to a sloppy defense and a possible injury. So make sure you do your road work and train hard during your rounds in the gym. Do the calisthenics listed in this chapter to develop strong arm and abdominal muscles so you can throw and withstand hard punches.

Whether your boxing training is for fun or for competition, your workout should be similar for both. A strong focus will lead to a rewarding result.

ROAD WORK (RUNNING)

Boxing is 90 percent stamina, which makes road work very important. Early morning is the best time to run, because the air is fresher and there is less traffic to contend with.

When you start running, start out easy. Run one to two miles a day. As you progress, you don't need to run for more than five miles a day or for more than forty-five minutes. Mix it up by doing wind sprints (short sprints with jogging in between), light shadowboxing (throwing punches as you run, with stops for combination punches), shuffling, and running backward. It is important to have fun. You want your run to be vigorous but enjoyable—not too hard, not too easy.

GYM WORK

Do the core of your gym work during the afternoon or early evening. If you work a nine-to-five job, train either during your lunch break or directly after work. Mix light days with heavy days and go to the gym four to six times a week, depending on the intensity of your workouts and your goals. Competitive fighters should train six times a week and run every morning. No matter what, always make sure you have a day off to rest and revitalize.

Once you are in a real boxing gym, your workouts will be dictated by a bell. The bell rings every three minutes, with a one-minute rest break between rounds. Under each of the following exercises I have included how many rounds you should work and the equivalent in actual minutes.

BOXING: The Complete Guide to Training and Fitness

BOXING WARM-UP

It is essential to warm up and stretch before every workout. Even if you are not working on a heavy bag or throwing punches, it still is important. Too many fighters become injured because they did not warm up properly, so take your time and work carefully. Start your warm-up from the top of your body and move down. Take nice deep breaths and relax. If there is any discomfort during this first part of your workout, stop and consult a physician.

Head Rolls

Slowly release your head downward and gently roll your head from side to side. Work smoothly, stay relaxed, and breathe. *Never roll your head back, jerk your neck side to side, or over stretch (ten times side to side).*

Shoulder Rolls

Slowly raise your right shoulder toward your right ear; now take it back, down, then forward and up in a smooth motion. Circle several times. Do the same on your left side, then switch directions *(ten times each direction).*

Big Arm Circles

With your right arm, slowly reach forward, then high above your head, then backward and down. Keep circling in a continuous motion. Switch sides, then switch directions *(ten times each direction)*.

Alternating Half Circles

Reach one arm forward and up, while you reach the other arm back and up in a half circle. Relax your arms and let them swing freely; you are simply swinging your arms in an exaggerated motion *(ten times each direction)*.

Trunk Rotations

Put your hands on your hips as you stand with your feet a little more than hip-width apart.

1. Circle your hips in one direction several times, then switch directions, keeping your upper body upright *(ten times each direction)*.

2. Maintain the same position as you make figure-eight patterns with your hips going in both directions *(ten times each direction)*.

BOXING: **The Complete Guide to Training and Fitness**

STRETCHES

Stretch only to a slightly uncomfortable point, then hold the stretch for a few seconds. Take long deep breaths and stay relaxed. **Don't overstretch. Pain is your first indication of overstretching.**

Shoulder Stretches

1. Interlock your fingers and reach forward through your palms, feeling the stretch through your shoulder blades.

2. With your fingers still interlocked, reach toward the ceiling, feeling the stretch through your palms.

3. Release your fingers, open up your chest, stretch, reach back, and release your hands down.

4. Interlock your fingers behind your back and stretch through your palms.

Do this sequence four or five times, taking nice deep breaths.

BOXING: The Complete Guide to Training and Fitness

Full-Body Stretch

1. Reach toward the ceiling with the fingers of your right hand and stretch through your whole right side, from the tips of your toes through your fingertips.

2. Switch sides and stretch all the way though your left side.

3. With both hands, reach for the ceiling and stretch through your entire body from head to toe and release.

Do each side once. Stay relaxed! Breathe!

Forward Bend

With your feet hip-width apart, bend at your waist and bring your hands down and forward, reaching your palms to the ground and bringing your chest toward your knees. Keep your knees slightly bent. Hold the stretch and take several deep breaths. When you are ready, slowly roll up, one vertebra at a time, until you are standing upright.

Do once.

JUMPING ROPE

Every boxer starts or ends his workout with jumping rope. It helps foot-work and coordination and is great cardiovascular work. Ropes are made of either leather or plastic. Leather ropes last forever but are slower and cost more. Plastic ropes are faster and cheaper but tend to break. Most ropes come in two sizes: eight-and-a-half and nine feet. Most adults will want to work with the nine-foot size. To find your correct size, stand with one foot in the middle of the rope and grip both handles. The tips of the handles should come up to your armpits. If the rope is too long, put a knot on either end until it is the proper length. If it is too short, you need to change to a longer rope. If you are jumping on a hard floor, make sure you are wearing the proper shoes, such as cross-trainers, for support and cushioning. Repeated jumping with improper shoes can cause Achilles tendonitis, shin splints, and other injuries.

Jumping rope should be done at the beginning of your workout to warm up or at the end of your workout for cardiovascular work. The best way to learn is to just do it. Your hands and feet work in sync; as your hands go down, your feet jump up. It is important to find your rhythm. Try jumping once per rotation of the rope.

Learn how to do the boxer's shuffle, which is like jogging while jumping rope. Start by jumping on one foot several times, then switch feet. Then jump four times on one foot, then four times on the other. Once you are comfortable with that, jump two times on one foot and two times on the other, then one time on one foot and one time on the other. Jump on the balls of your feet, shift your weight from side to side, and keep your jumps low to the ground to maintain a quick rhythm.

Jump rope for five rounds at three minutes a round, working through the one-minute rests *between rounds, or twenty minutes total.*

SHADOWBOXING

Shadowboxing should come near the beginning of your workout as part of warming up. You can shadowbox in front of a mirror, on the gym floor, or in the ring. You are not hitting a bag, but moving around the floor as if you are fighting an imaginary opponent. Shadowboxing is vital to learning good technique.

Start by getting into your boxing stance. Throw your jabs. As you get warmed up, throw one-two combinations and then add your left hook. As the rounds progress, add uppercuts to create more complicated combinations. If something does not feel right, repeat it slowly and conscientiously until it does. Start moving around, working on your footwork as you throw punches. Move your head from side to side, working defense as well as offense. Stay focused. Show intention in your punches. Don't get sloppy or lazy. Picture your opponent in front of you and throw solid, crisp punches.

Shadowbox for five rounds at three minutes a round, taking the one-minute rests between rounds, or fifteen minutes total.

THE HEAVY BAG

The heavy bag is the bag that you will use the most. You can learn all your punches on this bag. The best bags are usually hard-filled and made of leather. Hard-filled bags can be tough on your hands at first, but when the bag is broken in, it is great to hit. The firmness allows you to really pop your punches. Soft-filled bags are easier on your hands, but they can be so soft that they are like hitting pillows. They absorb so much of the impact of your blows that it slows you down and your punches feel sluggish. Many health clubs have soft-filled bags that are good for beginners, but if you are a serious boxer and have proper hand wraps and gloves, you will want to work on a harder bag. It's faster and you can get in more punches per round.

You don't necessarily need a trainer to hold the bag. You can control its movement with your jab and move around with the bag.

Heavy bag work should come after shadowboxing. You should be fairly warmed up by the time you begin working the bag, which means you have created a nice glistening sweat. Start with basic punches and gradually add power with each round. This will come naturally because as you get warmer you will be capable of throwing stronger punches.

1. Like shadowboxing, start by jabbing and finding your reach (your punch fully extended).

2. Add your straight right and work on one-two combinations.

3. In the second or third round, add your left hook and work in the jab-right-left hook combinations.

4. When you get your timing down, add your body shots.

As you work, plant your feet, throw your punches, and then move around the bag. After every combination, go back to your jab and move either left or right. Go in both directions, bobbing and weaving, slipping side to side, and counterpunching. From the fourth round on, start throwing your straight right, left hook, and body shots, like knockout punches. When the bell rings, throw a power punch to end the round strong.

Work the heavy bag for six rounds at three minutes a round, taking the one-minute rests between rounds, or eighteen minutes total.

FOCUS MITTS

Focus mitts are pads your trainer puts on her hands and holds as targets for you to hit. With focus mitts you can work on defense as well as offense. This is the closest thing to sparring without getting hit, and it is an excellent way to work on reaction timing. It may take a while to find your rhythm, but be patient; it is well worth the effort.

When working with your trainer, practice moving around the ring. Work on bobbing and weaving, counterpunching, and blocking and slipping punches.

Work the focus mitts with your trainer for five rounds at three minutes a round, taking the one-minute rests between rounds, or fifteen minutes total.

SPARRING

At this point in your workout, if your trainer thinks you are ready, this would be a good time to work in the ring with a sparring partner. If you are a novice, you must first spend at least four to six months developing your skills and timing on the heavy bag. Your trainer should start your sparring sessions out easy. Have patience; sparring is completely different from bag work and you may feel like a beginner all over again. Boxing is a highly mental and emotional process, and you want to develop your confidence slowly. If you are brought along too quickly, you may start to get hurt in the ring and become glove-shy (scared of getting punched and of throwing punches). If this happens it could set you back several months in your training. Let your trainer slowly build you up to harder and harder sessions.

If you work without a trainer, it is wise not to spar at all. If you do decide to spar without the help of a trainer, be very careful. You do not want to set yourself up to get beaten up in the ring. Work with someone you trust with your life. Start off slowly, then build up as your confidence grows.

Always spar with proper fitting headgear, mouthpiece, and groin protector. All necessary sparring equipment is listed on page 15.

In the beginning, work on your jab and set up for your straight right. Your sparring partner should not throw any punches, but should just work on his defenses while you get acclimated to working in a ring. You should not start working on blocking and slipping punches until you have had several sparring sessions and are comfortable with throwing the basic punches and moving around the ring.

Spar for two to four rounds at three minutes a round, taking one-minute rests between rounds, or six to twelve minutes total.

THE DOUBLE-END BAG

The double-end bag is a very important piece of equipment. You can work both defense and offense on this bag, and it can improve your hand and eye coordination. Called a double-end bag because it is secured on both ends by a cord or a rope, this round bag comes in various sizes. The smaller the bag, the harder it is to hit. At the top of a double-end bag is a rope that is attached to the ceiling, and the bottom of the bag attaches to a stretchy cord that hooks to the floor. The tension on this cord can vary from very strong to relatively weak. A bag with a lot of tension is faster and harder to hit, therefore much more difficult for a beginner. A large bag with medium tension is recommended instead.

The double-end bag is difficult to get used to. In the beginning you will throw many punches into the air, but keep practicing and eventually you will find the natural rhythm of the bag.

Double-end bag work should come toward the end of your workout. This is when you can start to lighten up. Stay loose and on the balls of your feet. Work on hand and foot speed. Move around the bag and work defensively as well as offensively. Parry the bag and counterpunch. Slip from side to side and work in both directions. Always counterpunch after a defensive move. Stay loose, have fun, and be creative.

Work the double-end bag for four rounds at three minutes a round, working through the one-minute rests between rounds, *or sixteen minutes total.*

BOXING: The Complete Guide to Training and Fitness

THE SPEED BAG

The speed bag is a rhythm bag. It develops hand-eye coordination, which is the same coordination used in blocking a punch. It is a teardrop-shaped bag that is attached to a wooden platform secured solidly into a wall. The platform usually can be adjusted up or down for the proper height, with the middle of the bag at eye level. Hit the bag with the side of your hand or the knuckles. It will bounce against the platform three times. Then you hit it again, creating a natural 1-2-3 rhythm. Working successfully with the speed bag takes time. As you start to get better with it, you can use different rhythms. Like the double-end bag, the speed bag is a very frustrating piece of equipment. Keep trying. It comes with practice.

The speed bag should come at the end of your workout. Find your rhythm and work your right hand first, then your left; then switch back and forth from one hand to the other. Stay loose and have fun.

Work the speed bag for two to four rounds at three minutes a round, working through the one-minute rests between rounds, *or eight to sixteen minutes.*

CALISTHENICS

Calisthenics consist of sit-ups, push-ups, pull-ups, and medicine ball work. Working with weights is required only if you are trying to build up muscle. In that case, you want to work with light weights at high repetitions to create long, lean, agile muscles.

PUSH-UPS

Push-ups with elbows tucked: Place your hands shoulder-width apart. Tuck your elbows in as you release down to the floor. Keep your chin up. Push up, with your elbows brushing along side of your body. *Do twenty.*

Push-ups with fingers pointing in: With your palms on the floor and
your fingers facing inward, bend your elbows outward as you release
down. Push up, keeping your chin up and making sure your back is
straight and your hips and shoulders are in alignment.
Do three sets of twenty-five to fifty.

Push-ups with one arm: With your feet and legs wide,
place your left arm directly underneath your chest, shift
your weight to the left, and lower yourself to the floor,
keeping your chin up. *Do five to ten on each side.*

PULL-UPS

You'll need a sturdy bar that is high enough off the floor so that your feet
don't touch the ground when you have a firm grip on the bar. Depending
on your body type do ten to fifteen pull-ups for three to four sets, more if
you are stronger. If you are a woman these may be difficult at first; therefore, start with fewer reps. *Try to do at least three sets.*

BOXING: The Complete Guide to Training and Fitness

SIT-UPS

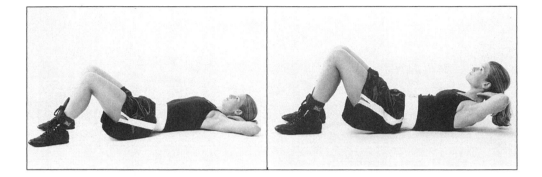

Crunches: Lie with your back on the floor, knees bent, feet on the floor, and hands behind your head. Using your abdominal muscles, roll up your spine until your shoulders and upper back are off the floor. Then, without pause, roll down vertebra by vertebra. *Do fifty.*

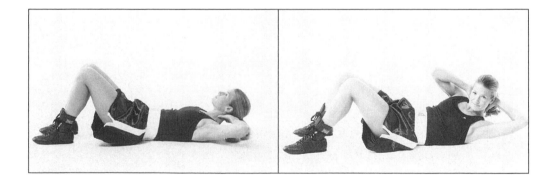

Crunches with a twist: As you roll up, add a twist at the end of your crunch. As your lower back comes off the floor, bring your right elbow toward your left knee. Then roll down. Repeat this on the opposite side. *Do fifty on each side.*

Hip raises with bent knees: With your feet on the floor, knees bent, and hands behind your head, use your lower abdominal muscles to bring your knees up to your chin; then down by bringing your heels to the floor. *Do fifty.*

Roll-ups: With your back on the floor and your knees bent, bring your knees toward your chest and your forehead to your knees with your feet and shoulders off the floor, then down. Keep your elbows wide. *Do twenty-five.*

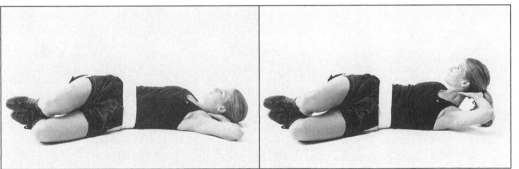

Side crunches: Roll to one side with hips parallel. With your elbows wide, bring your rib cage toward your hip, then down. *Do twenty-five each.*

Combining all of these abdominal exercises, build up to five hundred to a thousand in total repetitions.

BOXING: The Complete Guide to Training and Fitness

MEDICINE BALL (Working with a Partner)

Standing: With both people standing, the medicine ball is thrown back and forth. *Do twenty.*

One standing and one sitting: One person stands while the other person sits. The person standing throws the medicine ball to the person sitting. That person does a sit-up and throws the ball back. *Do twenty. Switch places.*

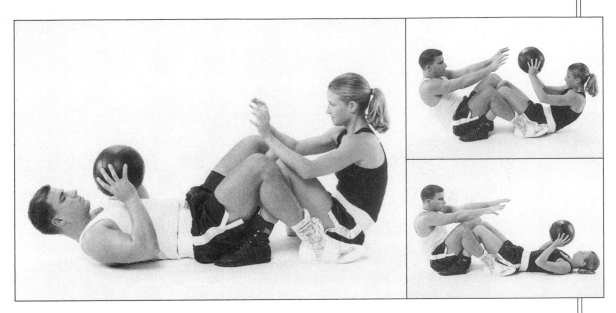

Sitting: With both people sitting facing each other, one person throws the medicine ball to the other person, who does a complete sit-up and then throws it back to her partner, who completes a sit-up. *Do twenty*.

Sitting back to back: With both people sitting back to back, the ball is passed around in a circle. *Go around twenty times in each direction*.

COOLING DOWN

Do one to two rounds of light shadowboxing (three minutes each round) and review lessons learned that day.

STRETCHES

Repeat the stretches that you did at the beginning of your workout and add the following:

Shoulder stretch: Reach your right hand directly across your body and interlock your right arm with your bent left arm. Drop your shoulder down and release through your shoulder blade, reaching through your shoulder. Reverse sides. *Do twice on each side.*

Quadriceps stretch: Standing straight, reach behind you and gently grasp your right foot with your right hand (use your left hand to hold a chair or a wall for support). *Very gently,* ease your right foot toward your buttocks with your knee pointing down to the floor. You should feel the stretch along the front of your thigh. *Be very careful not to overstretch.* Switch legs. *Do two reps on both sides.*

Standing calf stretch: Stand with your back leg bent and your foot solid on the ground. Extend your front leg straight with a slight bend in your knee and with the heel on the ground. Bend over and grab the ball of your front foot. Lean over and feel the stretch in your entire leg. Switch legs. *Do two reps on both sides.*

AFTER YOUR GYM WORKOUT

Take a hot shower, go home, and relax. You just did a very hard workout.

REST

Rest is absolutely imperative to becoming a good boxer. While resting, you actually build the muscles that were used during a workout. When you work out, you put stress on your muscles and then they heal and develop during rest. Never underestimate the importance of taking time off. You need to be as disciplined about it as you are about boxing. Rest and work go hand in hand, and improvement cannot happen without both. If you do not rest, you will not be able to sustain the edge needed for sparring and good bag work.

Your trainer should alternate your workouts with hard and easy days. It should look something like this:

Monday	Tuesday	Wednesday	Thursday	Friday	Saturday	Sunday
hard	hard	easy	easy	hard	hard	rest

or

Monday	Tuesday	Wednesday	Thursday	Friday	Saturday	Sunday
hard	easy	hard	easy	hard	easy	rest

If possible, sleep at least nine hours a night and try to have a twenty-minute nap sometime during the day. Remember, you are putting your body through a lot of stress and it must have time to heal.

DIET

When you first start to train hard, you will probably drop weight and increase your appetite. To maintain your weight, have a diet high in protein. Protein is essential during this initial phase because you will be developing muscles that you never knew you had. If you are trying to drop weight, cut down on carbohydrates, but still eat plenty of lean meat. Whether you are trying to maintain your weight, lose it, or gain it, cut down on sugar, salt, and fats. These will do nothing but slow you down in your workouts. No matter what, cut out all alcohol. Alcohol does not help you in any way to become a fighter.

Try to eat three hours before you work out so that your meal won't slow you down or upset your stomach. Eat the largest meal of the day after your gym work. Make sure your last meal at night is light and is eaten at least two hours before you go to sleep.

Again, your appetite will increase when you start working out. Don't starve yourself even if you are trying to drop weight. You need to maintain your energy for a hard workout and you should eat enough protein to develop muscle. You want to become lean and mean—not too bulked, and not too thin.

DRINK PLENTY OF WATER

Drink water before, during, and after your workout. Sip water after each round or every two rounds. Do not underestimate the importance of water, but do not overindulge *during* your workout or you might upset your stomach.

WORKING OUT FOR ONE WEEK

Monday—run two miles; boxing warm-up; jump rope four rounds; shadowbox four rounds; work the heavy bag six rounds, the double-end bag four rounds, and the speed bag four rounds; do calisthenics; cool down and stretch.

Tuesday—run four miles; boxing warm-up; jump rope four rounds; shadowbox eight rounds; work the double-end bag four rounds and the speed bag four rounds; do calisthenics; cool down and stretch.

Wednesday—run two-and-a-half miles; boxing warm-up; jump rope four rounds; shadowbox two rounds; work the heavy bag twelve rounds; do calisthenics; cool down and stretch.

Thursday—run one-and-a-half miles with sprints; boxing warm-up; jump rope two rounds; shadowbox four rounds; spar four rounds or work the heavy bag six rounds; work the double-end bag two rounds and the speed bag two rounds; do calisthenics; cool down and stretch.

Friday—run three miles; boxing warm-up; jump rope four rounds; shadowbox four rounds; work the heavy bag six rounds, the focus mitts four rounds, the double-end bag two rounds, and the speed bag four rounds; do calisthenics; cool down and stretch.

Saturday—run four-and-a-half miles; boxing warm-up; jump rope two rounds; shadowbox two rounds; spar four rounds or work the heavy bag six rounds; do calisthenics; cool down and stretch.

Sunday—get complete rest.

Maintaining this routine will get you strong muscles, quick reactions, and increased stamina.

BOXING IS A wonderful sport to learn. Start going to local amateur fights in your hometown. Not only will you be supporting young, up-and-coming fighters in your area, but you will start to see how some of the moves in this book are incorporated into a real ring fight.

By watching fights you might become interested in fighting yourself. Competition will add a whole new dimension to your workouts. No matter how old you are, you can still compete as an amateur. If you are over thirty-three, you will simply be put in the masters division. Whether you want to compete or not, I strongly recommend getting your amateur license. Write to:

United States Amateur Boxing, Inc.
One Olympic Plaza
Colorado Springs, Colorado 80909-5776
719-578-4506
http://www.usaboxing.org

Conclusion

Ask for an application for your area. If you are licensed and work out in a licensed gym, you should be fully insured in case of injury.

If you have never boxed before, start slow and find a good trainer and a gym you like. You are entering a whole new world that will test not only your athletic prowess but your personal fortitude as well. Boxers are a special breed of athlete that should be valued and admired. Have fun, enjoy yourself, and be careful.

Glossary

Ali lean Shifting your weight to your back foot and leaning back out of the way of your opponent's punch.

block A defensive move to fend off a punch delivered by an opponent.

bobbing and weaving Moving your head from side to side and making a U with your upper body. This is done by bending your knees, shifting your weight from side to side, and moving forward.

boxer A long-range fighter who is usually tall and works outside her opponent's reach.

clinching Tying up your opponent by interlocking your arms with your opponent's. Also known as *holding*.

combinations Several punches thrown in a row without pause.

counterpuncher A fighter who waits until his opponent is committed to throwing a punch before he throws his own.

Glossary

counterpunching Throwing a defensive punch after your opponent has thrown an offensive punch.

covering up Creating a protective shield with your hands up and your chin tucked in so you can absorb an onslaught of punches from your opponent.

double-end bag A light bag that is attached to the ceiling and the floor by a cord. It is used to build a fighter's hand speed as well as develop offensive and defensive moves.

ducking Bending your knees so you can go directly underneath an opponent's punch.

feint To fake a punch to confuse your opponent.

footwork The movement of your feet while boxing.

hand wrap A long strip of cloth that is wrapped around a boxer's hand to protect the bones of the hands and tendons of the wrists.

headgear Protective guard for the head. Used during sparring.

heavy bag A large bag suspended from the ceiling that can weigh from 75 to 150 pounds or more. It is used by boxers to work on combinations and footwork.

holding Same as clinching.

hook A punch that is thrown with your arm at a 90-degree angle and parallel to the floor. It is thrown to the side of your opponent's body, to either her head or torso.

infighter A forward-moving fighter who gets under his opponent's reach to throw hard punches to the body.

jab A quick, fast punch that is used to find timing and reach.

lead The first punch a fighter throws to set up a combination.

mouthpiece A piece of molded plastic worn in the mouth to protect the teeth and jaw.

parry To deflect an opponent's punch by swiping it to the side with the palm side of the glove, away from your face.

pivoting Shifting your weight to the front foot and pushing off the back foot to turn your body at a 90-degree angle to your opponent.

reach The full length of your punch.

referee Called the "third man," a referee makes sure both fighters follow USA Boxing rules and penalizes or disqualifies a fighter for continually breaking the rules.

road work Running.

rolling Turning your body in the same direction that a punch is going to minimize its power and deflect it off your arms and shoulders.

slipping Moving your head from side to side to avoid getting hit.

southpaw A left-handed fighter.

sparring Practice fighting with a partner. Usually a trainer is present.

speed bag A light bag attached to a suspended platform that is used to improve timing and hand-eye coordination.

stance The position of your feet while you are throwing a punch.

telegraphing a punch Unintentionally showing your opponent that you are about to throw a punch.

uppercut A punch delivered by either hand, palm up, thrown either to the sternum or to the tip of the chin.

Index

Index

Index

About the Author

DANNA SCOTT HAS trained Golden Glove winners and national contenders as well as total novices. She teaches traditional boxing techniques with an emphasis on aggressive offensive fighting. She is a licensed amateur and professional cornerperson and has been training amateur fighters for several years. She has worked in various boxing venues throughout the country including Madison Square Garden in New York City and the Cow Palace in San Francisco. She has also been highlighted in national magazines and on Lifetime Television and MSG Sports.

The author between husband-and-wife boxers Stephanie Rahm and Tom Orloff

To purchase videos by Danna Scott—*Boxing Training Basics, Boxing Training Advanced*, and *Boxing Ring Strategy*—call Century Martial Arts at 1-800-626-2787 or find them on the Internet at **www.centuryma.com**.